Sheep Station

Alan Trussell-Cullen

Australia • Brazil • Japan • Korea • Mexico • Singapore • Spain • United Kingdom • United States

Sheep Station

Fast Forward
Yellow Level 8

Text: Alan Trussell-Cullen
Editor: Johanna Rohan
Design: James Lowe
Series design: James Lowe
Production controller: Hanako Smith
Photo research: Michelle Cottrill
Audio recordings: Juliet Hill, Picture Start
Spoken by: Matthew King and Abbe Holmes
Reprint: Jennifer Foo

Acknowledgements
The author and publisher would like to acknowledge permission to reproduce material from the following sources: Photographs by ANTphoto.com/ Denis O'Byrne, p. 9 bottom; Australian Picture Library/ Paul A. Souders, pp. 4, 6, 7; Auscape/ Mike Langford, back cover, pp. 8, 12 bottom; Istockphoto.com/ pp. 14 top, 15 bottom; Photodisc, pp. 4-5; Photolibrary.com, pp. 15 top, 12 top/ Catherine Secula, p. 9 top/ Charlie Westerman, p. 13 top/ David Hannah, front cover, p. 1/ Neil Duncan, pp. 10-11/ Superstock, p. 5; Photos.com, pp. 3, 14 bottom; Stock Photos/ Masterfile/ R. Ian Lloyd.

ISBN 978 0 17 012521 5
ISBN 978 0 17 012513 0 (set)

Cengage Learning Australia
Level 7, 80 Dorcas Street
South Melbourne, Victoria Australia 3205
Phone: 1300 790 853

Cengage Learning New Zealand
Unit 4B Rosedale Office Park
331 Rosedale Road, Albany, North Shore NZ 0632
Phone: 0508 635 766

For learning solutions, visit **cengage.com.au**

Printed in Australia by Ligare Pty Ltd
7 8 9 10 11 12 13 21 20 19 18 17

Evaluated in independent research by staff from the Department of Language, Literacy and Arts Education at the University of Melbourne.

Sheep Station

Alan Trussell-Cullen

Contents

FINDING THE SHEEP

It is spring and time to shear the sheep on the **station**.
The farmers ride up into the hills to look for the sheep.
A big sheep station can have over 3000 sheep on it.
Sometimes, it is hard to find them all.
It can take two or three days to get them all together.

Many people help with the work on a sheep station. A big sheep station can have up to 50 people working on it.

Chapter 2

SHEEP DOGS AT WORK

The dogs on the sheep station have
a lot of work to do, too.
They help the farmers get all the sheep together.
This is called **mustering**.

Running Words 105

Sheep Dog Facts

Farmers have different dogs
to do different work.
A heading dog is good at making the sheep go
where the farmers want them to.
It looks at the sheep but does not bark.
A huntaway dog barks a lot.
It gets all the sheep together
and will catch the sheep that run away.
A handy dog can do the work
of a huntaway dog and a heading dog.

Chapter 3

SHEARING

The **shearers** shear the sheep inside the **shearing shed**. It is hard work, but a good shearer can shear 200 sheep in a day.

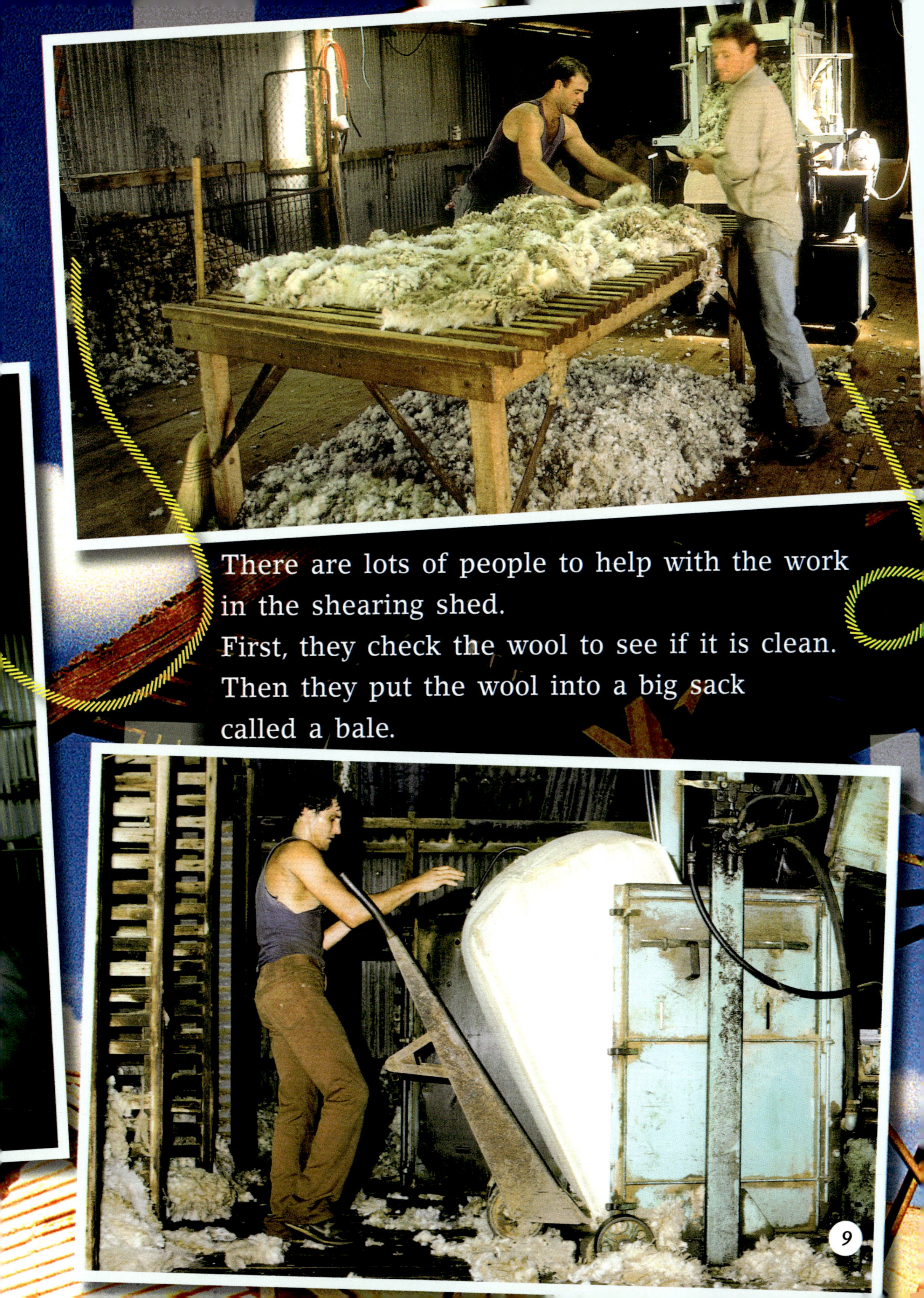

There are lots of people to help with the work in the shearing shed.
First, they check the wool to see if it is clean.
Then they put the wool into a big sack called a bale.

Back to the Hills

When the shearing is over,
all the sheep go back up into the hills.
They will now be cooler when summer comes.

Chapter 4

AT THE MILL

From the sheep station,
the bales of wool go to the mill.

At the mill, people clean the wool, dye it and spin it into yarn. Today, machines do most of this work.

What Is Made with the Wool?

Lots of things are made with the wool.

Most people have something made from wool at home.

Glossary

mustering	to get all the sheep together
shearer	a person who shears the sheep
shearing shed	a big shed where shearers shear the sheep
station	a very big sheep farm

Index